Chance Encounters
of a Literary Kind

Memoirs by Robert Day

Chance Encounters
of a Literary Kind

Memoirs by Robert Day

Serving House Books

Chance Encounters of a Literary Kind

ISBN: 978-0-9862146-8-4

Cover design by James Dissette

Cover photograph of New York Public Library by James Dissette

Serving House Books logo by Barry Lereng Wilmont

Published by Serving House Books
Copenhagen, Denmark and Florham Park, NJ
www.servinghousebooks.com

Member of The Independent Book Publishers Association

First Serving House Books Edition 2015

This book is dedicated to Mary Wood, Andre and Monique Kumela, Jane Alix, Walton Beacham, Phyllis Sipahioglu, Daglind Sonlet, Douglas Glover, Robert Stewart, and Kathryn Jankus Day

Ceci est la maison des amis de mes livres.

Books by Robert Day

The Last Cattle Drive (novel)
In My Stead (novella)
The Four Wheel Drive Quartet (novella)
Speaking French in Kansas (short fiction)
We Should Have Come By Water (poetry)
Where I Am Now (short fiction)
The Committee to Save the World (literary non-fiction)
The Billion Dollar Dream (short fiction)

When I am playing with my cat, how do I know that she is not playing with me?

—Montaigne

Contents

Exit, Pursued by a Bear: Introduction

Douglas Glover

Robert Day and I met something like 35 years ago in a University of Iowa classroom. He was the teacher, I was a student. He strode into the room and proceeded to the blackboard where he wrote, in large capital letters, from one side of the room to the other: REMEMBER TO TELL THEM THE NOVEL IS A POEM. Outside of class we got to know each other a bit. He was from Kansas but taught at Washington College in the east; summers he went west to a friend's ranch near Hays, where he kept a horse that had eaten his hat. Day once said, pressing the elevator button instead of climbing one flight of stairs, that if God had meant us to use stairs he would not have invented elevators. I was on the cusp of a truly disastrous relationship just then.

Day said to me, "Get out of there. For every day you spend with her now, it'll take you another year to get out of it." Ask me if I listened to him.

One afternoon we spent an hour kicking tires at a Jeep dealership. And one day he talked to me about the novel I was working on, a conference that must have lasted all of 20 minutes but somehow managed to open the novel and show me its hot, beating heart, which hitherto had failed to reveal itself to me. That was a lesson I did listen to.

Now, many, many, many years later we have congregated again through the magical intervention of the Internet and the online magazine I materialized called *Numéro Cinq*. We hadn't been in touch in years; we still haven't actually seen each other since 1981. But we continue to exert gravitational force upon each other's lives in ways that are astonishing and delightful. The long and short of it is that I began to publish Robert Day. A short story first. Later the story became a novel. I published the entire novel.

Then I published a memoir about his mother, a tender, sweet essay about her suspicion of the French, Day's love of Montaigne, and the summer she died while he was living in France.

Then Day invented a new form, the Chance Encounters of a Literary Kind memoirs, brief, whimsical, sometimes touching, reminiscences about his brushes (often friendships) with literary greatness. The first one he wrote and tried out on me was about the poets John Ashbery and Tadeusz Rozewicz. He didn't meet them; they met in his mind, and in a conversation with a friend over a kitchen table in Kansas. But the collision was sparkling in its reverent irreverence and the intuitions spawned in the erotics of juxtaposition. But it was also airy, gossamer-thin, a playful and informal thing, a little *jeu d'esprit* that took itself not very seriously, yet with flashes of seriousness and wit. Day asked me if I wanted more of these. He projected a series. He made a list. He wrote: "I'd like to keep the *Chance Encounters* real—that is, what I stumble into or on to as I lead my literary life; there should be x of them the rest of the year because I poke around in these matters often these days, and, like any fiction writer, stories (and chance literary encounters) happen to me."

I have my favorite moments. Day and Raymond Carver quoting Jack London back and forth to each other. Day's sweet evocation of the life-philosophy of poet William Stafford, who once advised his young daughter, "Talk to strangers." This is in an essay that goes on to ponder our current Age of Fear, the prevalence of surveillance, and our willingness to submit to precautions that cheat us human relations.

I also adore Day's piece on screenwriter Walter Bernstein, especially Day's expert interventions in an early script for the movie *The Electric Horseman*. Day being from Kansas, Bernstein considered him the expert on cowboys and horses. "Somehow Walter had learned the word hackamore (probably from an East Coast riding friend) and so I had to take the hackamore off all horses and put bridles and bits back in their mouths." And, of course, the "Exit, pursued by a bear" stage direction from *The Winter's Tale* that pops up unbidden and like fireworks in Day's essay on Sarah Palin and going to see a production of *Coriolanus*.

The buzzword these days for someone who wanders about poking idly into things (and being brilliant and witty about them) is *flâneur*. But when I read Day's essays I think, not of Walter Benjamin, but of the waggish early 18th century essays of Joseph Addison and Richard Steele and the journals they published, *The Tatler* and *The Spectator*, whose purpose it was "to enliven morality with wit; and to temper wit with morality." Day's essays are intelligent,

literate conversation at its best—all too rare these days—
written with aplomb in the author's trademark amiable and
self-ironic style.

Preface

Counting out the memoir on William Stafford and the essay Montaigne, I wrote the rest for the on-line literary magazine *Numéro Cinq.* The series began with lunch at Fred Whitehead's house in Kansas City, Kansas where indeed by chance I found on his table Tadeusz Rozewicz,'s *In the Midst of Life.* And also by chance I had brought along the latest edition of the *New Yorker* with John Ashbery's poem "Resisting Arrest" to show Fred. In fact, I don't much like Rozewicz, and Fred doesn't much like Ashbery, but we didn't draw pistols over it.

In Woody Allen's *Midnight in Paris*, he has Ernest Hemingway say that all writers are competitive. Which in Hemingway's case I take to mean "combative." I don't see myself that way. But then it is true that I don't read much contemporary fiction: Robert Cover when I see (gratefully) a story of his in the *New Yorker.* Julian Barnes as well. Mainly I think I am competitive with myself, like an only child on a Kansas farm will play himself in basketball, first being Bill Russell, then Clyde Lovellette. Nabokov speaks to this when he says he is his main reader in the circle of his lamplight.

I also got to thinking about the writers I'd met over the years: more accomplished in all cases than am I now, nor am to be. I liked them. They liked me. We knew that about one another. I never had a sense that my limited literary stature when compared to theirs made any difference.

Sorry, Hem. I don't box. I play one-on-one basketball with myself.

I could have written about others: Katherine Anne Porter, who once told me I needed to talk to myself in the voice of my characters while we split a pint of her Virginia Gentlemen in a seminar room on the very dry University of Kansas campus late one winter afternoon.

There was Anthony Burgess who found me via Secker and Warburg, my London publisher, and told them I wrote "...remarkably fine North American English." We met off and on as by chance we could, and once at a party where the host had a piano I fed Anthony American song titles from between the wars and he played them all with glee, singing as well: "A Small Hotel," "Dancing on the Ceiling," "The Way You Look Tonight," "April in Paris," "The Last Time I Saw Paris."

Beyond these, there was the poet Marvin Bell, the literary editor Ted Solotaroff (author of *The Red Hot Literary Vacuum*), and my Shakespeare professor, Charlton Hinman—about whom I have written elsewhere. And at Hollins College there was Eudora Welty who told me she'd declined the school's offer of a plane ticket or a driver to fetch her but instead took a bus. There are more stories on buses, she had said. George Garrett, her host that day, agreed. And there was, now that I think of it, George Garrett.

Finally, there is my mother whose literary business was her son, an only child trying to explain to her the necessity (if that's what it was) of going to Southwestern France to write about Northwestern Kansas. I wrote her eulogy for the *Washington Post Magazine* as a Mother's Day tribute; it was rejected as "…being too good to be true."

There is much talk these days about the nature of embellishment in memoir. My guess is I am among the guilty, but I would not be sure of evidence against me even if I could produce it myself. Have I jiggered time? Have I rearranged place settings at my literary tables? Had others say for me what I could not say so well for myself? The muse that calls on me as I write does not have a fact check "app" (whatever that is), so she is no use in this matter (and if she were, she would be useless in more important matters).

In the *Preface* to his short stories Hemingway writes: "…reading them over… you are always faintly embarrassed… and wonder whether you really wrote them or did you maybe hear them somewhere…" I know the feeling; many must have it.

What I like about these memories, and especially about my mother's eulogy, is how true they are.

Talk to Strangers and Stop on By: William Stafford

At the library of Congress in 1994 there was a memorial tribute to William Stafford, the brilliant American poet who, in 1970, had been what is now called the Poet Laureate of the United States.

There were the usual accolades: Bill Stafford was a poet whose plain language fitted his flatland Kansas sensibility. He was a man who thought peace (Stafford was a conscientious objector during World War Two) was good; war was wrong. There were other kind words. About the self-evident and the oblique stories in his poems. About those poem's gifted reticence. Then something extraordinary was said. One of his children, his daughter Kit I think, told us of her father's repeated advice to them as they were growing up: *Talk to strangers.*

I was Bill Stafford's student in the sense that I learned from him about writing and life: *Do it all and do it all now. The threshold is never so high as you imagine. The beginning may not be the beginning. The end may not be the end.* These aphorisms applied not only to his craft and mine, but to the way we lived. And there was a sense in what I learned from Bill Stafford that the two might not be easily separated.

Not far from where I live in Kansas (and about the same distance from where Bill Stafford grew up) there is a high school in a town of roughly a thousand that has a

18

video security system of which they are especially proud. I had been asked to be part of a literary program there (my talk was on Bill Stafford), and came to know about the surveillance cameras because I saw one posted in the room where I was speaking. Later, I saw the black and white glow of the monitors in the school's office. I watched as the system projected pictures of the gymnasium (empty on this autumn Saturday); various hallways (also empty); our meeting room (adults milling around drinking coffee and eating donuts); and finally a shot outside the school: the wide Kansas prairie as background, a small Kansas town in the foreground.

One of the school's officials and a parent stopped to say that you couldn't be too careful these days, what with Columbine and Amber alert. Bad things happen in schools. And out of schools. Better to be vigilant than be sorry. When they left, I could see them on the monitors as they walked across the buffalo grass lawn to where they were parked. They talked for a moment over the bed of a pickup truck, and then drove off, safe, I suppose, in the knowledge that someone might have been watching them.

Over the years Bill Stafford and I wrote back and forth: letters, post cards, copies of our work sent to one another with inscriptions. As he was one of the most prolific poets of the 20th century, I got plenty more of the latter than did he. But no matter how far apart we were, Bill in Oregon and me in Kansas or in Europe, he would sign off with something like "Adios" or "Cheers", and then, as if we were just across the pasture, he'd note: "And stop on by." My sense now is that when I'd get to him, windblown and dusty from the walk over, he'd want to know if I'd met any strangers on the way, and what stories they had to tell.

Have we become an America where it is stupid to give the same advice to our children that Bill Stafford gave his, and where *stop on by* means *please don't?* Have we come to believe that surveillance cameras in the high schools of tiny prairie towns will teach our students the eternal vigilance they'll need to live in towns beyond their own? Or in their own? What with Columbine and Amber alert. Or is the answer from Bill Stafford's poem *Holcomb, Kansas?*

> *Now the wide country has gone sober again.*
> *The river talks all through the night, proving*
> *its gravel. The valley climbs back into its hammock*
> *below the mountain and becomes again only what*
> *it is: night lights on farms make little blue domes*
> *above them, bring pools for the stars; again*
> *people can visit each other, talk easily,*
> *deal with real killers only when they come.*

Or are we all real killers?

There may be no reclaiming Bill Stafford's vision of America, but once upon a time, in his plain voice, didn't he speak for you?

Sarah Palin, Coriolanus and William Kristol

By design I am driving Barbara Mowat (who, along with Paul Werstine, is the editor of the *Folger Shakespeare*) to her Washington D.C. home on Capital Hill. We have been at dinner with journalist friends of mine where I shopped my theory that Sarah Palin is a plant of the Democratic Party, a deep, deep mole who was recruited as a college student when someone from the DNC saw her as Goneril in a production of *King Lear.*

What we have now is Sarah Palin as Rogue Sarah Palin, the woman who won the election for the Democrats in 2008 with her verbal gun-play, and even now looks through cross-haired scopes in search of anyone wanting to deprive Donald Trump of a tax break for his helicopter. Like Dustin Hoffman in *Tootsie*, Dame Palin will peel off her mask toward the end of the script—but not until Hillary has been elected President in 2016. Just you wait and watch.

"The Shakespeare Theatre Company is staging *Coriolanus*," Barbara says as we cut across D.C. "I can get us good seats. Would you like to go? A matinee. "

"I've never seen it," I say. I am trying to remember if I've ever read it. "Sure."

"It's probably his most political play," she says.

"In reference to my...?"

"Yes."

Barbara and I go back. She was the Dean of Washington College in Chestertown, Maryland when I was running a boisterous and politically incorrect literary center for student poets and writers. Barbara was amused. Most deans would not have been.

As we turn onto Connecticut Avenue I remember that I had read *Coriolanus,* among 13 other plays in a course called Shakespeare Rapid Reading—a play a week to the semester's end. *Coriolanus* was the final one, and now that my brain is flooding ('trickling ' is a better word) with the details of that course, I recall that if our professor was not puzzled by *Coriolanus*, those of us who drank our red beers at the Gaslight Tavern after class were.

Coriolanus had no great flaw, only a series of arrogant mistakes; no fall from grace, in fact no grace at all but a mean-spiritedness from the start that takes on different forms as the play goes along—much like his name. And because this was the sixties, those of us listening to Joan Baez on the jukebox in the Gaslight thought Coriolanus' trashing of the poor in want of food amounted to *Let them eat cake.* Our revolutionary mantra was: *Free Food and No Banking.*

"The forty-seven percent," I say out loud as we continue down Connecticut Avenue. "The Tea Party."

"What?" says Barbara.

"I was just remembering how Coriolanus got all bent out of shape because the poor wanted food. And what Mitt Romney said. And how the Tea Party attacked Obama over Food Stamps." We are quiet while I circle a circle. Twice, until I get off where I am going.

"Shakespeare calls the poor 'Plebeians,'" Barbara says. "And the nobles are the 'Patricians.' Coriolanus is 'bent out of shape'—as you put it—because the Plebeians' food riot won them tribunes in Rome's new Senate." Before she was a tolerant Dean, Barbara was a patient Shakespeare professor.

To continue the conversation I find myself hoping bits of flotsam from the play will rise to the surface after all these years: Something about Volumnia, Coriolanus' mother. Wounds from battle. A Kent-like character trying to bring reason to the action (good luck). A kid who rips up butterflies. Coriolanus as traitor. Death in the final scene. That's about it.

"Turn here," Barbara says, taking me off Connecticut before we reach Dupont Circle. "Otherwise you'll get entangled with traffic on Massachusetts Avenue." A woman who knows her way around texts and traffic.

"The play begins before Rome was Rome; have I got that right?"

"A city taking shape. Maybe the size of Washington. No empire. What it will become is up to Coriolanus. There is a scene toward the end where the Folio stage direction reads: 'He holds her by the hand, silent.' In that moment the fate of Rome is being decided."

I am thinking that the only stage direction I remember from Shakespeare is 'Exit pursued by a bear.'

"'Exit pursued by a bear,'" I say.

"*The Winter's Tale*," Barbara says.

Drive on McDuff.

The canard in recent years has been how utterly modern Shakespeare's plays are: Hamlet's introspection is our Vietnam syndrome. Lear's folly speaks to family values: what to do with a mad old father who won't give out the password to his mutual fund account? There is Othello and all that goes with being a Moor in white bread America; Lady Macbeth and the dark side of feminism. Between theme and scene we've got it covered. And all of it imported with its modernity intact from the early 17th[h] century to ours. Including *Coriolanus*.

Before we go to the Shakespeare Theatre Company production of *Coriolanus*, Barbara sends me the Folger edition of the play with the inscription: "For Bob, a Shakespearean in spite of himself."Such stuff are dreams made of.

Reading it, I was struck by how much Coriolanus and his play are alike, as if he had fashioned it himself to be so. Being modern is one thing, being Post Modern is quite another. Still, there it is: our anti-hero and his play both misshapen from that disproportionately long opening scene (is it the longest opening scene in Shakespeare, I wonder?) to a plethora of mini-scenes scattered throughout, without a romantic balcony one among them. Nor a Fool to name the folly of the future should the present be prologue. Only the thoughtful Menenius as a mediator, who, like Kent fails against raging internal storms.

Then there is the brooding nature of both the text and the character. No soliloquy down stage, but instead flashes of anger to tell us who he is, not that we know for sure who he is even if he claims such knowledge himself. It is not so much what Coriolanus does that defines him as what he won't do: show his wounds, for one; obey his mother, for another; reason when in need. The man and his play are defiant. Old fashioned 'form and content' gurgling up from my undergraduate studies.

I wonder where it comes from? Did our playwright get bored with the formula of his previous tragedies, replacing comic relief scenes with shards of black wit; dropping strong subplots that mirror main plots, then thinning out the plot itself until there is less of one than meets the eye? Even the memorable lines are few and not all that memorable: 'Bid them wash their faces and keep their teeth clean.' is no 'To be or not to be.' And 'Nature teaches beasts to know their friends' is not 'But, soft! What light through yonder window breaks? It is the east, and Juliet is the sun.' We Falstaffs at the Gaslight Tavern thought Coriolanus' 'The gods sent not corn for rich men only,' worth memorizing until we realized it was delivered with contempt for the poor. In the end (and all through the play) you get the sense that our author, like his character, is not going to show off. *Been there, done that.*

The play should have been a wreck to assemble because of its defiance at being well-wrought. And audiences are, after all, pulled along by what screenplay writers call 'rooting interest.' Other than the fate of fledging Rome there is not much of a home team to root for. But still it was compelling, partly because of the acting and sets—and the virile violence it all conveyed. (I wondered if I were the only one afraid Coriolanus might smash the fourth wall and march his wrath off stage toward Row 26, Seats 4&5). And watching it in Washington D.C, the political heart of our country, we were struck by how, as Barbara had observed, political it was.

"It's the extremes," I say to Barbara afterward.

"Yes," she says.

"Howard Baker as Menenius," I say. I am fishing for connections.

"He, too, would fail in times like ours," she says. "As would his wife."

"A brief on sore losers: George Will. Fox News. Lindsey Graham?"

"Yes."

"Obama?"

"He's not violent; he's not a traitor; he seeks common ground for common good, so no. But he won't show his scars, that's for sure."

"Not like Lyndon Johnson."

"Not at all."

"Nancy Regan as Volumnia?"

"Very funny."

"No Sarah Palin?"

"Too bad for you," she says.

We talk on like this walking in the sunshine toward my car and discover equations are not easy to make; the play on stage became more a brew than a math problem. However, there was that moment Barbara had mentioned, the scene where Coriolanus holds his mother's hand, a scene which I had spotted and nudged Barbara to make sure. When I bring it up, she says:

"Because the play takes place when Rome was vulnerable to the many tribes and armies nearby, had the Volscians, led by Coriolanus and Aufidius, been successful in defeating Rome, then Western history would have been a different story than the one we know."

I have lost track of where I parked my car in thinking about what I am hearing. Barbara continues:

"Shakespeare shows Coriolanus impervious to the requests for mercy from Rome: he is determined to destroy the city. When his mother arrives, he starts out just as impervious to her pleas. Then something happens inside Coriolanus, and Shakespeare renders the moment that saves Rome not as a soliloquy but with that stage direction 'He holds her by the hand, silent.' This allows Rome to survive and seals Coriolanus's fate (as Coriolanus well knows). I can't think of any moment in drama quite like it."

I see my car down a side street and steer us that way.

"Maybe it is not the politics we have these days that makes the play political" I say, "but fear of the politics we might one day have."

"That too," Barbara says, as I open the door for her and she gets in. On the way to Capitol Hill I ask:

"Who was your Shakespeare professor?"

"Fredson Bowers, at the University of Virginia. And yours?"

"Charlton Hinman," I say. "We were told he was a great textual scholar."

"He was," says Barbara. "He also studied with Fredson Bowers at Virginia."

"A chance encounter between us after all these years."

"What fun," she says.

Getting to Barbara's house I explain my new theory that, like Sarah Palin, Dan Quayle was a deep mole for the Democratic Party, both of them unwittingly brought to America's political theater by the Sal Hurok of the Conservative Movement, a.k.a. William Kristol of the Weekly Standard.

"But the Republicans won," says Barbara.

"Somebody didn't read the stage direction toward the end," I say.

"Friends are Never Even":
Jack (aka) John Barth

We met in the late 1970's when Jack and I tried to convince one another that I should be the Director of the Johns Hopkins Graduate Creative Writing Program. I was then teaching at Washington College, in Chestertown, where it turned out I stayed. But from those first days when I toured the Hopkins Writing Seminars, meeting the faculty and students, Jack and I became friends because of—as Montaigne writes—who he is and who I am.

Robert Day and John Barth

Not long after our pas de deux at Hopkins, Jack called to say he would be coming to Chestertown (where he and Shelly had recently bought a house) the following Friday and would I join him for lunch? Agreed. It was to be the beginning of scores of Friday lunches.

Where we met that first time I do not remember, but I do remember that our talk was rangy, ebullient, and exclusively literary. Well, not exclusively literary because from the first we'd swap jokes—Jack beginning with a series of Hillbilly pig jokes when he learned I had studied a stint at the University of Arkansas, and me in trade Ranch Jokes imported from West Jesus Land, Kansas where I live part time. The second thing I remember is that someone must have spotted Jack (a new book of his was just out with his photograph appearing in the papers) and took our picture.

Avid readers of John Barth will know that those Friday lunches were because of, or resulted in (or some formulation thereof) his three collections of essays. *The Friday Book*, *Further Fridays*, and *Final Fridays*—the latter volume including a piece published in *Granta* titled: "The End? On Writing No Further Fiction, Probably." Toward the conclusion of that essay I am mentioned as an anonymous co-conspirator to his muse: More on this later.

Thus our literary lunch Fridays commenced and continued. Not every Friday, but many over the years until Jack stopped teaching at Hopkins and was more often in Chestertown, in which case our Fridays turned themselves into Wednesdays or Mondays—or *encore*, a real Friday itself.

In the beginning, one of us would pay the lunch tab then the next time the other way around, even though sometimes we'd get confused. At one lunch I said I thought it was my turn but Jack said no, it was his, and he insisted. To which I said, I'm not sure we're even, to which Jack replied: "Friends are never even." And about that time, once again, someone took our picture.

"What do you think the caption will be?" I had asked Jack. "You first," he said. "Nationally famous author lunching with unidentified man," I said. "I'll pass," he said, but in the moment of silence between us, I thought that his fertile and fervent literary imagination could have made an entire novel out of my minimalist caption.

What my friend has accomplished with his fervent imagination is the creation of a world of fiction unlike any other American writer. And the landscape of that world is immense: From the early realistic and nihilistic novels, *The Floating Opera* and *The End of the Road*, to the faux historical novels, *The Sot Weed Factor* and *Giles Goat Boy*, and then changing course to *On with the Story, Letters, The Tidewater Tales, Lost in the Fun House, The Last Voyage of Somebody the Sailor*, and back to *On with the Story, Coming Soon, The Development*, and his most recent book: *Every Third Thought, A Novel in Five Seasons.*

Jack's writing is not so much a landscape of fiction as an Ocean of Story. But writers are not unique just because of the breadth of their oeuvre. There has to be something else. An editor we shared at the *Washington Post Magazine* called that "something else" *The Pyrotechnics of Prose.*

It is as if my friend's muse is a character in his fiction,

at least the muse that is his gift of language. Surely some critic has noticed the jazz improvisations in Jack's writing: I have. Those are what we who write call *invention*. It comes from where we've been coming from in the paragraphs before. And the chapters before that. And it arises from where we've come from as readers: In Jack's case, back to Lawrence Sterne in English and further back than that in ancient languages and oft told old tales told on a thousand and one nights. All of these he spins into tales of his own, with his own voice and muse doing the spinning. Like Joyce and Nabokov and Garcia Marquez and Italio Calvino, he conjures a maelstrom into his own Ocean of Story. He is Tradition and the Individual Talent. And fireworks at sea.

We had lunch again the other day, a Wednesday as Zeus would have it. Before we met I read the *Granta* essay in which Jack muses that his muse is not musing these days. In it he writes "A writer-friend from Kansas who knows about water-wells informs me of the important distinction between dry wells and *gurglers* which may cease producing for a time but eventually resume; he encourages me to believe I'm still a Gurgler."

Our lunch was at Evergrain in Chestertown, Maryland. We took an outside table to enjoy the sunshine. After all these years we tell many of the same jokes, but sometimes I tell one Jack has told me and take credit for it, and Jack does the same. He doesn't recall his early Hillbilly pig jokes and I need to be reminded of my Kansas parrot joke. In this way at least we are even. Then we talk about Philip Roth and how he has recently resigned from writing fiction

—-as opposed to?…But neither of us mention it. About this time, someone takes our picture.

Between that first photograph and this one I have taught thousands of students at Washington College, and those students are sending their children, and in some cases, their grandchildren, to the college. Mothers and fathers and a few grandmothers and grandfathers were now coming back for Parents' Weekends and Graduations. And having lunch out. Some stopping to reintroduce themselves.

"What's the caption?" I ask Jack.

"*Locally famous professor having lunch with unidentified man,*" he says. To which in the small silence between us I think: Lucky me to have had an oeuvre of Friday lunches with my friend talking books and telling jokes. And lucky all who are avid readers of muse-inspired American literature to have had John Barth with his firecracker prose going off like St Elmo's fire in his Oceans of stories.

As we walk down the street to our cars, I ask Jack if he is the one who told me the aphorism that as we age, *Sex goes, memory goes, but the memory of sex never goes.*

"I think you told me," he says.

"Let's both take credit for it," I say.

"Co-authors?"

"We'd be even for once if you don't mind."

"My pleasure," he says. In this he speaks for me.

John Ashbery and Tadeusz Rozewicz

"... that old woman who / is leading a goat by a rope / is more necessary / and more precious / than the seven wonders / of the world/any one who thinks and feels / that she is not necessary/is a mass-murderer ..."
Tadeusz Rozewicz, from *In the Midst of Life*

"...Ah nerts, / ...this guy's too much for me."
John Ashbery, from *Self –Portrait on a Convex Mirror*

By chance: I was reading John Ashbery's poem "Resisting Arrest" in the April 30th , 2012 issue of the *New Yorker* at Fred Whitehead's dining room table in Kansas City, Kansas.

"Look at this," I said.

"Look at this," Fred said, and handed me a copy of Tadeusz Rozewicz's New Poems.

If the world of political religion were only as generous and accommodating as the world of poetry we could all live in un-interesting times, unless you count reading verse that makes nothing happen (in both senses of Auden's famous phrase) as interesting. Which I do.

That these two poets are popular and splendid in ways beyond their received definitions (Ashbery, the modern master of *Ars Poetica* yoked to back stories; Rozewicz, the

34

voice of poetry as assertion), is evidence that some small part of what passes as modern civilization is free from cant, hypocrisy, and contempt—not to mention drone strikes, suicide bombers, female circumcision, and the mass murders of innocents by tyrants fat and skinny.

Robert Day and Fred Whitehead

An Ashbery poem—at least like "Resisting Arrest"— begins in the middle of ... what? And goes from there with interruptions by folk mostly inside the poem. Exits and entrances pursued by themselves. The stanzas are verbal brush stokes (in French coup de pinceau, as I recently learned from writing a short story) that are being applied (even as we watch) to the making of abstract expressionist verse. It is what William Stafford called the "adventure" of writing. But for most poets we don't watch the adventure in process. Ashbery's process is his poetry.

He told a cheering crowd the infighting was over

at least for that day. They had more affairs
to remember than just that one time. Why,
he went over it and that was that. Plethoras
to be announced, etc. You're telling me.

That is not the first stanza of "Resisting Arrest," but why not? Begin anywhere, to borrow the title of Frank Giampietro's astonishing poem from his book by the same name (Alice James Books).

However, Rozewicz is narrative. His strength is the absence of mystery about who is talking, and about what:

Tuesday April 23
the 113th day of 2002

today
I have the day off

I listen to the rain falling
I read poems
By Staff and Tuwim
(From: " luxury")

An adventure of sorts, but it does matter where we begin: elsewhere and everywhere in *New Poems*:

On the road
of my life
which has been straight

though sometimes
it disappeared
round the bend
of history

there were whirlings

on the road of life.

(From: "on the road")

Rozewicz's is the road taken, and there are plenty of folk along the way:

Midnight

I read Checkhov smile at him
What a kind good man
He must have loved people…
"ich sterbe" he said and passed away

(From: "The poet's other mystery")

Pound
was right
not to be fond
of capitalists and money lenders
he sought to drive the merchants
from the temple …

P.S.
too bad Pound never finished
Mein Kampf
Before he started extolling
The Fuhrer

(From: "Too Bad")

We meet people in Ashbery's travels as well, but mostly they seem residents of the poem:

A pleasant smell of frying sausages
Attacks the sense, along with an old, mostly invisible
Photograph of what seems to be girls lounging around
An old fighter bomber, circa 1942 vintage.
How to explain to these girls, if indeed that's what
*   they are,*
These Ruths, Linda, Pats and Sheilas
About the vast change that's taken place
In the fabric of our society, altering the texture
Of all things in it?

(From: "Mixed Feelings")

What both poets have in common is the *allure* of their language. In Ashbery it is mystery coupled with glamor. In Rozewicz the language is attractive because of his minimal bluntness. And both poets are diarists; it is just that Ashbery's entries are coded, and Rozewicz's are not. That, too, is part of their respective allure.

"Poetry is what gets lost in explaining it," I say to Fred, sort of quoting (I think) Frost.

"Talking about literature is as natural as breathing," Fred says. Eliot.

I am trying to remember what Philip Larkin said about all this so I can keep our verbal duel going, but my mind shoots blanks some days—and this is one of them.

"Globed fruit" comes to mind, but I know that is not Larkin. To cover my tracks, I read two poems out loud, one from each:

philosopher's stone

this poem
should be put to sleep
before it starts
to philosophize
before it starts

to cast about
for compliments

summoned to life
in a forgetful moment

attuned to word
to glances
it seeks deliverance
from a philosopher's
stone

passerby walk on
don't lift the stone

under it a tiny white poem
naked
is turning
to ash

Paradoxes and Oxymorons

This poem is concerned with language on a very plain
     level.
Look at it talking to you. You look out a window
Or pretend to fidget. You have it but you don't have it.
You miss it, it misses you. You miss each other

The poem is sad because it wants to be yours, and
     cannot.
What's a plain level? It is that and other things,
Bringing a system of them into play. Play?
Well, actually, yes, but I consider play to be

A deeper outside thinking, a dreamed role-pattern
As in the division of grace these long August days
Without proof. Open-ended. And before you know it
It gets lost in the stream and chatter of typewriters.

It has been played once more. I think you exist only
To tease me into doing it, on your level, and then you
     aren't there

Or have adopted a different attitude. And the poem
Has set me softly down beside you. The poem is you.

Fred and I are quiet for a moment wondering (at least I am) can anyone not know to whom these poems belong? Then we talk more about language, and how Ashbery's vernacular becomes literary in spite of itself:

The difficulty with that is
I no longer have any metaphysical reasons
For doing the things I do.
Night formulates, the rest is up to the scribes and the
    eunuchs.
From: *The Preludes*

As for Rozewicz and his plain style, at the end of "learning to walk" Jesus edits him as follows:

then He came to a stop
and said
friend
strike out one "big word"
from your poem
strike out the word "beauty"

Which apparently Rozewicz did, as it does not otherwise appear.

By chance: It is also true that The Library of American's edition of Ashbery's *Collected Poems 1956-1987* and Archipelago Books' edition of Rozewicz's *New Poems* are

41

both elegant in binding and design—albeit, like the poets themselves, in different ways. Which brings me to (in fact) the opening stanza of "Resisting Arrest."

> *A year and day later the wolf stopped*
> *by as planned. He made conversation*
> *about this and that but you could tell*
> *from the way he favored his gums that all was not*
> *well. Later the driving pool shifted.*
> *I had no idea that you were planning*
> *to stage an operation but it's all right*
> *this time. Then I read your account and*
> *was dully impressed, right at the edge*
> *of the sea where the land asserts itself.*

"What's that about?" Fred asked.

"Beginning anywhere," I said. "And maybe the end of 'No meaning except in things.'"

"William Carlos Williams," Fred said.

"'Globed Fruit' Archibald McLeish," I said.

"I think so," Fred said.

Mavis Gallant (1922-2014)

It was through Phyllis Springer and Goksin Sipahioglu, the owners of the celebrated photo agency SIPA press in Paris, that I met Mavis Gallant. This was in the 1980s. Mavis lived in the apartment next to Phyllis and Goksin on the left bank near Boulevard Montparnasse, not far from 27 rue de Fleurus. In that same apartment building in those days lived the Czech novelist Milan Kundra, with whom I had no encounter.

I had been staying in Paris above a couscous restaurant on rue Xavier Privas that I shared with fullback-sized cockroaches. In those days I drove a yellow Duex-Chevaux I named Colette. I would park her where I could, changing places in a failed attempt to avoid parking tickets, but at least not being towed.

Some days I'd buy a lunch from *un marchand de rue* and, with a bottle of *vin de pays*, take my meal on Square du Vert Galant, a point on l'Ile de la Cité where I'd watch the *bateaux mouches* on the Seine. One such lunch I saw a barge going up the river packed with cars; Colette was among them—in fact, on the bow, like a figurehead.

It took three days of my poor French and 300 Francs to free her from the Fourrière, a kind of dog pound for cars. Later, just before I left Paris, I put an AV sign in the windshield and sold her to a sous chef of Café de Palais on Place Dauphine. Adieu: Colette.

Sometimes Phyllis and Goksin would invite me to join

them for dinner at a restaurant where they were habitués. It was at one of those meals that I met Mavis: La Marlotte? Brasserie Lipp? Closerie des Lilas? Probably La Marlotte, as that was not far from where they all lived.

It was at that meal that Christiane Amanpour stopped to say hello to Gokskin and Phyllis; she had worked for them at SIPA before she turned to television reporting.

"He is a great photographer," she said to me, putting her hand on Gokskin's shoulder. "Do you know that?" I said I did. "And Mavis is a great writer," she continued. I said I knew that as well.

I had, like almost any American author who writes short fiction, read Mavis's stories in the *New Yorker*. Along with Salinger and John Cheever in those days, you could earn multiple graduate degrees in creative writing by reading these authors. At one point I typed (on a manual typewriter, it was that long ago) parts of stories from all three to see what they had accomplished, and how they did it. I learned, among other things, what a fine sense of local detail these writers had: Salinger for the parks and subways of New York City; Cheever for the upstate suburbs with roaming lovers and Labrador Retrievers; Mavis Gallant for the rues of Paris (her stories were their own *Plan de Paris*).

Also at that first dinner, Phyllis asked Mavis if she had walked that day. Paris has many rainy days, and that had been one of them.

"Walk every day in Paris," Mavis said. "It is how I fetch my stories. Not to do so would be impossible."

Years later, when she was crippled by arthritis and diabetes, Mavis's agent made her a Christmas gift: a year's worth of taxi rides so she could continue fetching her stories.

I imagine her with the notebook of her writer's mind open through her eyes as she has the driver take her toward Place de l'Odéon, and then down where the students rioted in 1968. The next day the taxi is driving her across the Seine toward the Hotel de Ville in the 4th, past the apartment buildings and cafes and art galleries of her characters, and beyond: to Pere Lachaise in the 20th—all the time Mavis not looking where she had been in her previous work, but where in her mind's eye she would be setting new stories once she got back to her writing.

In the years that followed our first dinner, Mavis and I would eat *entre nous* at restaurants that her characters and mine frequented; she would order from my fictional menu, and I would order from hers—both being true to our characters. There were more characters of hers to feed than mine. *Tant pis.* At least I ate well, and in her company had bright and witty talk.

At one such lunch (at Le Cherche Midi I think because it was open on Sunday), she lectured me that I was not a writer because I did not make my living as one; beyond that, I taught creative writing, which is not how writers learn. I said I knew the latter from reading her stories. She smiled.

As if to compensate for her rather pointed points, she ordered a split of Chateau D'ay (the appellation delighted her given the company), and toasted the quality of my fiction: *Très amusement*, which was high praise, as she thought herself a comic writer.

Très belle:

To Mavis Gallant, after all these years I toast both the woman and her fiction, as if the two can be separated which, had you watched her walking through Paris in the rain (as I did one day on my way to join her for lunch, her head turned here and there to see what would become the facts of her fiction) you know is, thankfully, impossible.

Dave Smith

By design I was to introduce the poet Dave Smith on December 4th, 2013 at Rockhurst University in Kansas City, Missouri. By chance an ice storm struck Mississippi where Dave lived and he could not make it. By design he returned to give his reading at Rockhurst in September; by chance I could not be there. Those of us who write as much for pleasure as for profit try not to waste words; better to recycle them, to wit:

Dave Smith and I have been friends for almost thirty years which might surprise him because we met only four or five years ago and since then have passed only a few hours in each others' company.

We did not grow up together; his brother did not date my sister, and we did not get in a fight about it; we did not hunt quail together with me out-shooting him (or the other way around) neither of us boasting of it but instead agreeing it was good practice to feed the quail heads to the dogs. We did not swap lies at the local tavern, nor tell raw jokes back and forth, the same ones again and again over the years, my favorite being about the Ozark man who feeds his pigs apples and Dave's being an especially reprehensible one about a hillbilly taking his daughter to the doctor for birth control pills.

And we have not grown old together, the two of us at a high school reunion a few years ago in either his Virgil

Cain's south or my West Jesus Land, Kansas, re-calling that in our youth we'd talk about breasts and buttocks but now we talk about stove-up bowels and government bonds. How is it then have we been friends all these years? By the power of the 17th century metaphysical poet's ability to yoke the mechanics of compasses with the sublimity of love I will explain.

Not that Dave would know this, but I first met him when he was in Utah and I was in Paris. A left bank book store (not Shakespeare and company) had a display of American literary magazines, and I bought two or three to take back to my apartment in the couscous quarter. In those literary magazines I read a number of poets whose work I knew (and knew in person as well as in print) and some I did not: Dave Smith was among the latter in both regards. But instead of being just a poet whose poetry I had not read, he became a poet who sent his poems directly (and especially) to me via a literary cosmic connection established well before the Internet.

Surely all of us who read have had such an experience: Bill Stafford wired me poetry from the early sixties on— well before we met. William Maxwell and J.D. Salinger hailed me from New York City. Evan S. Connell sent me high signs from New Mexico years before Paul Newman and Joanne Woodward became Mr. and Mrs. Bridge. Henry Green (not Graham Green) found me sitting on a bench in Washington Square's Greenwich Village, Mary Travis a bench away. Paul Bowles got in touch from Tangiers while I was in California at the No Name bar in Sausalito listening to Tom Leher sing *Poisoning Pigeons in the Park* on the jukebox. As Dave Smith writes of the poet Richard Hugo: "His poems spoke to a listener that I did not know was in me; an ear I didn't yet know listened."

Remember when Holden Caulfield says that when he reads a good book he wants to call the author. That's what it is like. Only in reverse: Dave Smith called me in Paris and we began over the years a magical literary conversation. Not that Dave Smith knew (Or maybe he did and just never told me). Which reminds me: Garcia Marquez got in touch from Macondo; Elizabeth Bishop from the *New Yorker*; Amos Tutuola from Nigeria; Elizabeth Bowen from Dublin; Jean Rhys from Paris; and in Kansas City at the Westport Inn where I was sitting at a back table having a red beer, Anderi Bely hailed me from Petersburg at the suggestion of Valdimir Nabokov who, in the early sixties, had sent Dolores Haze in her "circular skirt and scanties" to my night stand at the Window Dunn's farm house in Lawrence, Kansas.

The list is long; the world is round, the conversation everlasting. Dave Smith spoke to me; I listened.

The Dave Smith I met on rue Xavier Prive in Paris that summer wrote thin, long one stanza poems; more elegy than story. Others were short and taciturn. Not quite lyrics, they were less songs than small bore single shots to the squirrel of our heart. I imagined him trim as his poems, and short. Over the years, his gift expanded, and so did his poetry. To read Dave Smith now is to read one of America's fine narrative poets. To read his prose, as in his book *Hunting Men* (in which the Richard Hugo piece is included), is to read one American's fine literary essayists.

Metaphors and similes happily abound in both. This is Dave's description of three coyotes running ahead of a car at night in a snowstorm, taken from his poem "Christmas Concert, With Violin."

> *They took the road oblivious as saints. Soon flecks of*
> *   ice*
> *   like metal shavings, then blizzard. We followed.*
> *Snow spooled, slammed, like treachery, hiding those*
> *   shadows.*
> *As I gripped the unknown way, snaking, we'd*
> *see them in and out, crossing a creek, clattery bridge,*
> *   the new*
> *milk-blue on their backs like royal robes.*

Ever since the *Iliad*, the narrative poem and repetitive similes have cohabited in verse. But in our time, not since A.R. Ammons, has a poet used metaphor and simile with the descriptive power of Dave Smith. Or, as he writes of Ammons, "he felt the weight, metaphysical and back bending, of snow."

Such accomplishment is not much admired these days. We look for less length in our verse, less story, and a lot less of what one confessional poet told me was "the dead white whale poet still lingering among us." I was tempted to point out that whales, even dead ones, don't "linger." And like Oscar Wilde I did not resist.

In the end however, what must be admired, at least for the sake of what is left of our Republic of Letters, is Dave Smith's poem itself. *Christmas Concert, With Violin* is huge, running 28 stanzas to nearly 200 lines. And those stanzas are an unrhymed version of rhyme royal (think Chaucer) where the stanzas are sometimes rooms, and sometimes rooms that adjoin one another to deepen the scene while carrying along the story. In this way, *Christmas Concert, With Violin* is both dramatic and narrative, all in pursuit of an adventure—not unlike the classical epics. I know of no other poem like it.

What friends who are writers do is make literary gifts to one another: slices of scenes, bits of dialogue, stories, all as a way of saying: I can't use it, maybe you can. Better to recycle than even compost. Dave, here's one for you from me:

Years ago, even before we became friends, I was a student at the University of Arkansas Writer's workshop in Fayetteville where, on the local television news one evening, there began live coverage of a murder on Magazine Mountain. Someone had been "butchered into body parts," as the reporter told us. Now the search was on to find the "whole fellow, who ever he was." To that end the sheriff, a man named High Hat Hal, had called upon the local hunters to lend a hand, in this case their dogs. Each evening for about a week, I would tune into the television news to learn what body part had been retrieved.

"What do we have today?" The reporter asked.

"One of Ed Earl's pointers drug back most of a leg," High Hat answered. "It was River Johnson's coon dog that found it, but coon dogs are not much on fetching. You know River Johnson?" He was the reporter's shoestring cousin.

As the week went by, the other leg came in, then one

hand and most of both arms—-but not the body itself, which High Hat opined had been either digested and passed by bob-cats or tossed into the West Fork to float down to Simpson's ox-bow where the turtles would "nibble it clean." As to the head, again it was River Johnson's coon dog that bayed at it, but Texas Tom's half-breed retriever who brought it back so badly chewed they'd have to send it to Little Rock to see who it was.

"That dog always was hard-mouthed, " said the sheriff.

With all the body parts more or less accounted for, it was left to the following week for the Sheriff to report that they'd found the murderer, a man not yet named but charged. His wife had turned him in after she'd freed herself from his chaining her to a washing machine, then running the spin cycle with a lump of wet blanket on one side to shake the devil from her innards.

"He was apparently given to Jesus," the Sheriff told us. The body parts had been the wife's lover.

Dave Smith, my friend all these years, make a huge poem of it, from that I'll write a screenplay. Like James Dickey, you can be the sheriff; I'll be the reporter. We'll need to find a High Hat, some dogs, and an actress willing to be chained to a washing machine. But in the end, how about the two of us walk out of the final frame like Rick and Louie in *Casablanca*? Only I want to be Humphrey Bogart for reasons having to do with Ingrid Bergman. Dave: The story is yours. As is my gratitude for your friendship.

Ray Carver

It was in Iowa City where I first met Ray Carver. He was then teaching at the Writer's Workshop. I don't recall what I was doing there, maybe being interviewed for the kind of job Ray had: you teach one semester or two, and then someone takes your place. (In fact I did that a few years later.) Or maybe I was just passing through to see my friends Marvin Bell and Jack Leggett. Speak, memory?

Somehow, some place, for some reason, Ray asked if I'd drive him to the Iowa City airport. Sure. By this time I'd read a number his stories in *Esquire* (not knowing then about the controversial cuts that had been made by Gordon Lish, the fiction editor). In those days Ray was drinking. He drank on the way to the airport, offering me a pull. Thanks, but no thanks. Keep the bottle for me, he said as he got out of the car. Sure.

In the car I talked; Ray did not. Or at least not much. I told him what I thought about his fiction, especially *Fat*, using the two terms that in those days were applied to his work: "K Mart Fiction" and "Minimalist Fiction," what *Granta* called "dirty realists"—that's those Brits for you. Reading his stories, I said, he had taught me a few things. You don't need much teaching, he said, and tried the bottle on me a second time. I'll put it on your desk in EPB, I said. Thanks, he said.

I also asked where he was going. For some reason I remember it was a Wednesday afternoon. You could teach either a Monday-Wednesday morning schedule at the workshop or a Tuesday-Thursday morning schedule. Ray had apparently picked Monday-Wednesday for reasons that I would learn later might have had to do with his flight that day.

Chicago, he said. Chicago? He said nothing more.

Frank Martin uncrosses his arms and takes a puff on the cigar. He lets the smoke carry out of his mouth. Then he raises his chin toward the hill and says, "Jack London used to have a big place on the other side of this valley. Right over there behind that green hill you're looking at. But alcohol killed him. Let that be a lesson to you. He was a better man than any of us. But he couldn't handle the stuff, either." Frank Martin looks at what's left of his cigar. It's gone out. He tosses it into the bucket. "You guys want to read something while you're here, read that book of his, The Call of the Wild. You know the one I'm talking about? We have it inside if you want to read something. It's about this animal that's half dog and half wolf. End of sermon," he says, and then hitches his pants up and tugs his sweater down. "I'm going inside," he says. "See you at lunch."

This passage is from Ray Carver's story "Where I Am Calling From." I will explain later.

The next time Ray Carver—in fact the next two times— came into my life were through his editors, one being Michel Curtis, the fiction editor of the *Atlantic Monthly*, and the afore mentioned Gordon Lish of *Esquire*. In what order is also now lost to my apparently speechless memory.

At Washington College where I once taught we would bring in poets and writers for the students, but I thought a good literary editor might helpful as well. That had been my case when I was a student and the University of Arkansas MFA program brought to campus Ted Soloratoff of *New American Review*. It was in this spirit that I had invited Mike Curtis, fiction editor of the *Atlantic*.

In advance of his arrival, he sent me a copy of the magazine in which Ray's new story, "Cathedral," had been published. It was not at all like the Ray Carver stories I had read in *Esquire*. It was long, very long, and there was nothing K-Mart about it. But there was something else: it rambled as a matter of design. Not shamble, because there was nothing awkward or clumsy about its pace. If Carver's *Esquire* stories were tight in their telling, this one was loose. But in its fashion, beautifully telling.

At lunch that day with Curtis and students I thanked him for the *Atlantic* and said how much I enjoyed "Cathedral," but that it was long for a Carver story. It is neither long, nor short, Mike said, it is the right length for the story. His answer seemed blunt, as if there were reasons behind it I did not understand.

We then talked about length (as opposed to brevity) in short fiction, with Melville being part of the conversation, along with Katherine Anne Porter and J.D. Salinger. But I kept thinking how quickly Curtis had made his point about Carver. I refrained from asking about the absence of the K Mart stores in "Cathedral," much less "dirty realism."

It was a few years later (or earlier?) that also in the sprit of bringing an editor to campus that I invited Gordon Lish, the fiction editor of Esquire. The students at Washington College had a literary house for themselves where they would give readings, host visiting writers, hold a salon among themselves, publish literary magazines and, using a warren of rooms, write novels and stories and poems and plays. All through the house were framed posters of those literary folk who had stopped by: Edward Albee, Gwendolyn Brooks, William Stafford, Allen Ginsberg, Toni Morrison, Joseph Brodsky, John Barth , Katherine Ann Porter, Anthony Burgess, Lawrence Ferlinghetti, Richard Wilbur, John Ashbery, Diane Wakoski, and more. *The Washington Post* called their house the Carnegie Hall of Literary Readings. They put it on a T-shirt.

It was the custom of the literary students who inhabited the house to decide if the visitors were worthy or not. If not, the poster would be hung upside down. Very few were, but apparently they thought Gordon's visit (consisting of conferences, classes, and a public lecture) was so poor they turned his poster to the wall. Done.

Well, not quite done. Some of the students pointed out that while Lish was of little or no help to them with their writing, through him, Ray Carver had been. Not that I knew this until I was told later that everywhere Gordon went on our campus (to a student reception for him; in classes; in the conferences he had with students over their work), he brought up Ray Carver: What a fine writer Carver was and that one way to develop as a writer was to read with a writer's eye authors you admire. Ray Carver, Gordon Lish had asserted, will teach you by what he has written. Type out passages you like from his stories, Gordon told them, and he will teach you more than your creative writing teacher (that would have been me).

After some debate, and after the students began reading Carver, a new vote was taken and Gordon got turned around. Still upside down, but at least no longer a blank on the wall.

What those students learned from Ray Carver was probably what I had learned: his restraint in describing or delineating a character and in this way giving the character a chance of his own; his candor about the grim faults of those he had created; his half open- ended, endings, as if a door is left ajar. I owe him.

The second time I met Ray was with Jack Barth at a bar in Baltimore to get something to eat before Ray was to give a reading at Johns Hopkins that evening. Ray was not drinking, Jack had said by way of introduction. I nodded; Ray nodded back. I wondered if he had remembered me from Iowa City. I didn't mention it; nor did he. We talked books and writers. I mentioned Ray's use of Jack London in "Where I Am Calling From." He told me had learned a lot from London, but not about drinking. That he had learned on his own.

In the pause among us, I asked Barth how he learned to be a writer. It was a failure at being a jazz musician, he said. And you? he asked me. In fact it was from Jack London, I said. How so? asked Ray

I read "To Build A Fire" for a course in American Literature and when I went to class the professor explained that the story was a Man-Against-Nature story. He explained that for fifty minutes. There are Man-Against-Man, Man-Against-Society, and Man-Against-Nature stories. The next class the professor explained that sometimes nature wins, sometimes man wins ... and so on ... for another fifty minutes.

Ray said he'd heard that lecture as well.

Somewhere in the haze of those hundred minutes, I said, I found myself thinking how much I liked the writing in the story. The language of it. Shouldn't that count for something in an English class? Not that I knew then what could be said about the language. But when I went back to my dorm room and read the story again the writing seemed splendid in ways I could not name so that in order (I now suppose) to understand what I admired, I propped the book up beside the portable Royal type writer my mother had given me before I went away to school and typed out the first long paragraph which I then memorized:

Day had broken cold and gray, exceedingly cold and gray, when the man turned aside from the main Yukon trail and climbed the high earth-bank, where a dim and little-traveled trail led eastward through the fat spruce timberland. It was a steep bank, and he paused for breath at the top, excusing the act to himself by looking at his watch. It was nine o'clock. There was no sun nor hint of sun, though there was not a cloud in the sky. It was a clear day, and yet there seemed an intangible pall over the face of things, a subtle gloom that made the day dark, and that was due to the absence of sun....

Before I could finish, Ray took over:

This fact did not worry the man. He was used to the lack of sun. It had been days since he had seen the sun, and he knew that a few more days must pass before that cheerful orb, due south, would just peep above the sky-line and dip immediately from view.

He had been there before.

It was years later, and it was either Jack Leggett or Connie Brothers at the Iowa Writers Workshop, who told me that they thought Ray had been flying back to a college teaching job in California only to fly back later over the weekend to take up his position at Iowa. Not that anybody knew the story at the time. Or maybe they did. It seemed possible because it seemed out of a Ray Carver story.

Walter Bernstein

In 1977 Walter Bernstein was nominated for the Academy Award in screen writing. We met that same year at the MacDowell Colony in Peterborough, New Hampshire. To him I became "The Kansas Kid," sometimes shortened to "The Kid."

The movie was the Marty Ritt film, *The Front* staring Woody Allen. I had not seen it, nor did I know much about film scripts, and I knew nothing about Bernstein's accomplishments: *Fail Safe* and the *Molly McGuires* among other movies.

The other writers at MacDowell at that time included Lucy Kamasar (who had recently integrated McSorley's Old Ale House in the East Village); the poet and playwright Honor Moore; Milton Klonsky (who would win a McArther Award the following year); Iris Owens, who had just published *After Claude*, Mary Higgins Clark, the author of *Where Are The Children*, and a George X , working on his second book about Russia (I cannot, even with the help of Goggle find him, nor obviously recall his last name, even thought he loaned me his house on Ibiza the following year. Madness.)

I had just published a novel set in the west and in a moment of youthful vanity, I gave a copy to the MacDowell library where Walter checked it out. For what reason I would soon learn.

Walter Bernstein, Robert Day, and the producer Bert Leonard

MacDowell in those days was (and maybe still is) a gift of time and place for writers. You could stay up to about six weeks; they furnished you a small cabin where you could write and even stay over night if you didn't want to use the dormitories, also provided. Around noon a handyman arrived with lunch. My cabin (and I guessed others as well) had a fire place and when the man who brought you lunch saw that you'd used your stash of wood from the front porch, he brought you more. As I was there in January, I went through more than my share. It was the custom of the country that only the wood-and-lunch man was to stop by your cabin, and he never came in, nor even knocked.

For dinner you went back to the main hall where many of us gathered in a large room (also with a fire place) for drinks. I don't remember if we brought our own (I think we did) or there was a bar set up. Maybe there was a bar. There was much quick-draw and rapid-fire talk about politics and art, much of which (being who I was then) left me behind. I remember Iris Owens saying she had once worked for Maurice Girodias's Olympia Press in Paris. Her job was to edit the first draft of *Lolita*. I thought no one had edited Nabokov, much less *Lolita*.

"Oh," she said. "It was a mess of motels going all across the country running to 600 pages with the two of them entangled in the sheets every ten pages. I'd cut motels by states: there went three in Ohio, there went four in Illinois, there went all of Kansas." (And here she looked at me because Walter's name for me had gotten around). I believed her at the time.

The one subject that was off limits was our writing— the day's work that just ended, or whatever project was in progress for the stay. As I had never been around so many accomplished authors I missed the chance to hear them on their work. And how I understood I was not to ask came about because one evening at drinks I said to George X: "How goes it?" To which there was a collective silence, then: "It goes."

"Hey, kid," Walter said to me one evening at dinner. "I read your novel. Very good. Would you read a draft of my screenplay? It's a western and I'm a furtive Jew from New York. What do I know about cowboys?"

Walter was then writing *Electric Horseman*, not for Robert Redford, but for Steve McQueen who, it turned out, was about to die. When that happened the studio sent the project to Redford who fired Walter. But all that was to happen later. For the moment, Walter wanted to know what I knew about horses and cattle and cowboys. I was flattered. Sure, I said.

A few days later at dinner Walter gave me a copy of the script made from the MacDowell Xerox machine. Mark it up, he said. Or put lines down the side where I'm getting things wrong. Then we can talk. Sure, I said.

I had never read a movie script. There was "Ext." and "Int." Also "Cut To" and "Back To," with sometimes "Continuous." There were numbers running down the page which I took to indicate scenes. There were some (but not many in Walter's script) camera shots. Flush left on the page were descriptions. Sometimes accounts of what the actors were to do, sometimes of the setting. In between and indented, was the dialogue. I had no idea how I could be of help, but I knew I wanted to.

If you want to see Walter from those days, rent the Woody Allen film *Annie Hall*. You have to go all the way down the reel (to use Walter's term from before DVDs) but there he is, standing outside a movie theater with Woody Allen, Diane Keaton, and Sigourney Weaver. Walter is Annie's date. The script might have read: *Scene 47: Ext. Movie Theater. Alvy with unidentified woman; Annie with unidentified man. Gestures. VO (Voice Over)*:

I did run into Annie again. It was on the upper West side of Manhattan. She had moved back to New York. She was living in Soho with some guy. When I met her, she was dragging him to see "The Sorrow and the Pity"...which I counted as a personal triumph.

As to Walter's script, at first I found myself so mesmerized by the form that I didn't read it with care the way Walter wanted me to: But yes, there was confusion about horses, sometimes they were horses, then they were stallions, then they were mares (when in fact they were probably all geldings; the stallion star of the movie added later). I had to untangle bridles from halters; I had to take horns off cows, and change cows to steers (with or without horns, but I thought unless they were Texas Longhorns for show instead of ranch cattle, they had probably been de-horned.)

Somehow Walter had learned the word hackamore (probably from an East Coast riding friend) and so I had to take the hackamore off all horses and put bridles and bits back in their mouths. I also added lead ropes otherwise Robert Redford and Willy Nelson (in the final version) would be tugging horses (or mares or stallions) along by their halters, unless they were using reins attached to bits and bridles, which in two scenes at least they were not. Saddle blankets were fine. Stirrups as well. Saddle horns, yes. Chaps, ok, but we called them leggings. Spurs, fine. But from what I could tell they were never needed. Still, the audience probably needed them. Most of this was description and while I felt comfortable making those changes, when it came to dialogue, I was less sure of myself. However, I did without hesitation make one change: Walter had written a Willy Nelson line as: *Tonight I'm going to find myself a little Keno girl who can suck a tennis ball through a garden hose.* My rewrite (which, as it turned out, did not get me screen work) was: *Tonight I'm going to find myself a little Keno girl who can suck the chrome off a trailer hitch.* Arthur Laurents, eat your heart out.

"Thanks, Kid, "Walter said at dinner a few days after I had handed back the script. "I guess cowboys don't play tennis."

In this way, to paraphrase a bit dialogue from another movie, there began a beautiful friendship. But that was to be further down the reel for the two of us; in the meantime, it was the next week or so that Walter learned he'd been nominated for an Academy Award in screen writing which meant his picture was all over the papers, including *New York Times* that MacDowell subscribed to, plus various local papers when it was discovered that Walter was in residence at MacDowell.

I remember there was a toast in front of the fireplace one night. Then as well, pats and handshakes and cheek kisses over dinner as folk stopped. Our two person table grew chairs. Walter seemed pleased indeed.

About this time I got my first royalty check and I thought I'd like to share it with Walter by taking him to dinner. There was supposed to be a good place to eat in Keene, not far away: the Red something (Lion?) Inn. It will turn out that it is owned by a former student of mine from the college where I was then teaching. Not only was he the owner, but the chef as well.

"Sure, Kid. Thanks," said Walter. "But I have friends coming up in a few days, would you mind if they joined us. My treat." Fine I said, but insisted the bill would be mine. "Then I'll leave the tip," he said. "We'll use my station wagon." I made a reservation for four in my name.

Why Walter didn't tell me his two guests were Diane Keaton and Diane Carroll I don't know, nor did I ask. He might have meant to surprise me, but it didn't seem that way when we all met in the large hall, Walter saying to the two Dianes, this is Bob Day, he's helping me the Steve McQueen script. Bob this is … and … We all shook hands, although Diane Carroll gave me something of a hug and noted that it was about time Walter got the recognition. Then off we went out the door, bundled up in coats and sweaters against the New England January. I wanted to look back to see who was staring after us, but I did not. Grace under pressure.

At the Red Lion Inn, Diane and Diane go in first followed by Walter and me. The restaurant is busy. A pretty receptionist asks for a name. Four for Day, I say. From the kitchen toward the back I hear the voice of my student: "Day? My god, it's Bob Day." Imagine the reaction shot he saw when the two Dianes looked my way and Walter smiled.

Montaigne: A Way of Knowing as a Way of Life

Each summer and into the early fall, my wife, the painter Kathryn Jankus Day, and I take up residence at L'Etang, a 16th-century farmhouse on the estate of Michael de Montaigne just outside the village of St. Michel de Montaigne. The farmhouse sits in a valley near a pond below the Montaigne castle—a huge Disney-like 19th-century Loire valley imitation built after a maid set fire to the original castle in order to steal some jewelry. Or so the local story goes. Montaigne would be skeptical.

Montaigne's tower (where he wrote his essays) did not burn, and to this day you can take a narrow, circular stone stairway up to his round study where there sits a full-sized cloth mannequin of Montaigne himself. He is arranged as if reading the facsimile of the Bordeaux edition of his essays on the table in front of him.

Above this faux Montaigne are carved into the ceiling beams his beloved quotations from the ancients: *I don't understand. I am in doubt. (both from Sextus Empiricus) among more than 50 others: The judgments of the Lord are a vast abyss (Psalm 35); There is much to be said on all matters, both for and against.* (Homer, *The Iliad*).

It will bring you luck (again, according to local lore) if, during your visit to Montaigne's tower, you see on the stairs—or in the study itself—a black and white cat. The cat's name is Balzac. He was once our cat, a lost-and-found kitty we rescued from a poplar woods near St. Michel de Montaigne, a woods we have since named Bois de Balzac. My wife and I not only have our patois, we are the ones who started the story about spotting Balzac in Montaigne's tower bringing good luck. We believe in local lore.

Balzac on Robert Day's Mother's Typewriter

Montaigne's famous inquiry is persistent: What do we know? As is its modern corollary: How do we know? The first question was Montaigne's motto: *Que sais-je?* The second concerns our age of "expanding information," superhighways of information that race in an infinite number of lanes around the earth on cosmic beltways, complete with clover leafs and exits—Paris, Rome, Athens, Bombay, Hong Kong, Los Angeles, Chicago, New York, St. Michel de Montaigne, Bly, Kansas—all going faster by far than "break-neck speed," a phrase my mother would use to describe cars that passed our two-door Champion Studebaker as my father drove the R&P speed limit *(Reasonable and Proper)* on the roads of rural Kansas. Where are they going at "break-neck speed?" my mother would wonder. What madness is it? my father would reply.

Where are we all going at our 21st-century cosmic pace?—a pace that is not only to be contrasted with the R&P limits of 1950s Kansas roads, but with the walk-along rate of the Dordogne River that flows in the valley below Montaigne's tower: past the village of Lamothe, Montravel, then west to Castillon, Branne, Libourne and Fronsac—after which it joins the Gironde near Bourg. Then to sea. Where is the strong brown god of the river going? At what speed? Are we flowing with it? What do we know?

Does it mean something to how we know that it would have taken Montaigne four days on horseback to follow the Dordogne to Bourg and back in order to learn—and return with—the news that the grape harvest along the Côte de Bourg was just as bad as it had been for the Côte de Castillon? Does it make a difference to what we know that my father had to drive to see my uncle (who had no phone) to tell him of a death in the family? And to return with my uncle who wanted to stay with us that night because, as my mother said, he was feeling "mortal,"—and that that was the first time I had heard that word and was afraid to ask its meaning. Is there a ratio of speed to knowledge? Of information to knowledge? Of information to ignorance? Which of these ratios are literal? Which are inverse, ironic? What do we ever know? Seeing Balzac brings you good luck. If you say so.

I like Montaigne's way of thinking. In college I came to study him—as perhaps we all did—as the *père* of the essay. He was a master of "form." There were forms of literature in those days: novels, poems, short stories, essays. We were taught that the French word *essai* meant "to try," "to attempt." I don't remember any of us asking what we were to "attempt" when we took to writing our own essays; but over the years, it has occurred to me that in the main we are to try to think. Not so much to "reason"—as if an essay were a pudgy syllogism—but to think in a contemplative way, a tentative way. An essay as a walk along a road taken in search of a discovered thought provoked by a singular image: the black bird in the cedar limbs just as it is beginning to snow—and is going to snow.

In this way we let our words discover our reason. Is it a way of knowing? Maybe. Is it a way of knowing everything? Maybe. It is a way of knowing yourself, then, to wit Montaigne: "There is nothing so contrary to my style as continuous narrative." Walks with stops as digressions. Not a four-day, but a six-day trip to Bourg and back if on the way you ride your horse up the steep hill to St. Emillon and consider what there is to see. The Dordogne in the valley below. Someone on horseback riding toward Bourg. An essay on the move. The essay as a form of life. A way of knowing as a way of life.

A Mother I Cannot Find Again

My mother always wanted to live in a French Provincial house—but the house she imagined was in Fairway Manor, Kansas not in rural France. And her idea of "French Provincial" was not a southwest peasant Perigord but a Midwest suburban ranch. A shake shingle roof, wide soffits, and something called "weeping mortar" could turn a Frank Lloyd Wright Prairie House into a domesticated Mansard. Decorate the inside in late fifties chartreuse drapes and upholstery, put identical lamps on identical tables on either side of a three cushion couch (with a matching "coffee table" in front--on which you never had coffee, and in a living room in which you did not live), and you were in my mother's Midi.

"I don't know why you have to leave America," my mother said when I told her I planned to settle in France. "How am I going to call you if I need you?" We are sitting (for once) at my mother's coffee table. I have come on a surprise visit over a May weekend that has lifted the ban on the living room.

"I'll write out all the numbers."

"They'll be in French," my mother said.

"French numbers and American numbers are the same," I said.

"You're talking," she said. My mother had a way of teasing me that I was never sure about.

"I'll call you," I said.

"I'll be here," my mother had said. "But write me as well. You can't reread a phone call."

"Yes, mother."

"Do you speak French?"

"Un petit peu."

"What does that mean?"

" 'A little bit,'" I said.

"You can tell me other French words when you call."

"Five a phone call and after a year you'll be speaking French," I said.

"I should live so long."

"Bobby" Day and His Mother

My mother was suspicious of Europe, especially of France. Not that she was ignorant of foreign countries. Because my father had worked for TWA, we traveled when I was growing up: Paris. Rome. Venice. London. And a few car trips as well. I remember a long drive from Athens to Paris along the peaceful Adriatic coast of Tito's Yugoslavia, complete with a two-day stop in Joyce's Trieste.

And not that my mother was the "Ugly American" of those days. She traveled with patience and modesty, and with the understanding that if she did not always appreciate the local customs that was more her problem than others. Still, it did not suit her in Paris to eat hard rolls in the mornings, nor to drink wine at lunch, nor for the stores to be closed from noon to two—nor for dinner to be served at eight in the evening.

"It is bad for the digestion," she would say. "You'll just get fat and lazy eating so much at night and then going to sleep on a full stomach. And the lunches they have! With wine. And corks in the bottles. No wonder they have to take a nap." It was my mother who insisted that we book reservations at our Paris hotel restaurant for six. We ate in lonely splendor. And then took a long walk along the Seine afterwards.

"That's better," she had said. "Look at Notre Dame. The name means 'Our Lady.' The French are Catholic. Tomorrow we go home." Home was Fairway Manor, Kansas. Weeping mortar. A privet hedge. Anne Page bread from which she made "French Toast" on Sundays. And dinner at six, with wine—my mother drank Mogen David. No corks. My father had a Jim Beam before dinner. A Coors afterwards. On Fridays two Coors while he watched the fights.

But even given her relative patience with foreign travel, my mother was still wary of it. There was the water problem. The money was difficult to figure. Venice had an odor about it. In Athens they spoke Greek. In Paris it rained.There were menus to read and misunderstand (in northern Italy she ordered what appeared to me then—and even now in my mind's eye—to be the stuffed intestine of a small mammal). The traffic was impossible. Especially in cities where her assignment was to be the navigator to my captain father.

"We are at via Vicenza and Polizia," said my mother as we wound our way in and around Rome one day in desperate search of our hotel. We had just come back from a two-day trip down the Almafie drive.

"That can't be," said my father.

"Now we are at Via Vicenza and Gelato," said my mother.

"'Gelato' means ice cream," I said from the back seat.

"'Polizia' probably means 'police'," my father said from his Captain's seat. When under pressure my father would resort to understatement.

"There's the train station," my mother said. "Does that help?"

"We're looking for Piazza Navona," my father said. "Our hotel is just off the Piazza Navona."

"We're at Piazza Maggiore," said my mother, looking up from her map, then down, then up. "Take the first left." Which my father did, going a number of blocks the wrong way up a one-way street against a full orchestra of Italian horns.

"I don't think this is right," said my father.

"Oh dear," said my mother. "Now we're at Via de Serpenti and Gelato." In Rome all roads lead to ice cream. Or to the Polizia—who stopped us just as we exited into Roman sunshine of some fountained circle—and then waved us on when they saw that my mother was an American housewife lost in her map.

"Oh dear."

"When we get to the hotel may I get an ice cream cone?"

"Just what are you going to do in France?" my mother had asked that May Sunday.

"Live," I said. How else to explain to her what I was not sure I could explain to myself.

"Not like the French, I hope," she said. "Promise me you won't eat late. You'll just get fat and lazy. Or drink wine for lunch. And tell the truth when you write me, not like those stories of yours. The things you make up."

"I won't promise," I said. "But by this time next year, you can come and see for yourself. I'll pick you up at the airport. You'll be speaking French."

"I should live so long," she said. "Now where is it you are you going to be?"

"Southwestern France," I said. "Far from Paris."

"Do they still have those hard rolls?" she said. "And what about the water?"

"The water is fine," I said. "And yes they still have the hard rolls. But I eat *pain au chocolate* for breakfast."

"What's that?"

"You don't want to know."

"You must eat cereal for breakfast," she said. "Even in France. And remember cheese constipates. Eat salads with dinner. Prunes will help."

"Yes mother."

"I don't see the sense in it," she said. "Show me on a map exactly where you're going to live so I know where to call when I need you."

"Yes, mother."

I got out the map of France and southern Europe I had brought along for her to see where Bordeaux was, and where St. Emilion and Castillion were, and where the tiny village of St. Michel de Montaigne was—for it was in St. Michel and on the former Montaigne estate that I had made arrangements with Armel, a friend of mine, to restore an old farm house in exchange for living there. Until the basic work was done I would be staying in Armel's guest house in the village itself.

"Have we ever been there?" said my mother as she looked at the map, and the place on the map I had circled. "Did we go there with your father?"

"No," I said. "I have been there, but you haven't. However the three of us drove up through Austria from Athens, then on to Paris." And I showed her the route we had taken.

"Where did I order the inside of the possum?" she asked. "You remember the time I ordered the inside of the possum?"

"I do," I said. And I pointed to northern Italy.

"Do you remember the time in Rome when I kept telling your father we were at the corner of Via whatever and ice cream," she said.

"I do indeed," I said.

"Those were good times," she said. "And do you remember how your father took us to Alfredo's after we finally found the hotel, and that Alfredo served me the pasta in his own bowl with those golden spoons."

"Yes."

"And when the violinist came to our table your father asked him to play "Come Back to Sorrento," because that was the day we came back from Sorrento and how scared I was of the road." She is looking at the map and with her finger finding these places on it.

"I remember that as well," I said.

"Your father was very patient with me," said my mother. "Now tell me again, why are you going to France?"

"It is a doctor for you from America on the phone," Armel says. It is the middle of the night. He has come over to the guesthouse to wake me.

Over the summer I had made it my habit to call my mother every Sunday. In this way I have told her of my life in France: How the water is safe to drink; that I have named the swallows nesting at the farm house I am restoring; and about Hooter, a Dame Blanche that flies out of attic each evening at dusk. I have not told her that I drink wine with corks in the bottles.

She wants to know about the weather and if I am eating my cereal. And salads. And prunes. I tell her about the trips I make with Armel in his Deux Chevaux, and that its name means "two horses," and that the French word for ice cream is *glace*, and the word for street is *rue*. I have written her as well, but not as often as I should have. *You can't reread a phone call* echoes in my head after all these years.

As summer faded and September came on, I tell my mother about the grape harvest, and how I am helping at the Montainge estate to pick the grapes that will be made into wine, and that I will have the owner sign a bottle for her that will be her present when she visits me next May. I tell her that we will use Armel's Deux Chevaux and ride to Castillion and have lunch at the Hotel des Voyageurs and drink wine from a bottle that had a cork in it—and afterward, we will have *glace* from a pastry shop I know down the *rue* were the ice cream is rich and smooth.

I should live so long, she had said on the phone the Sunday before Armel came to the guest room to wake me.

Bob Day's Gossip: An Afterward

Dave Smith

Years ago I when I was an inveterate frequenter of used bookstores, I bought odd books and I sometimes read them. In that process, I came across *The Last Cattle Drive*, a novel by a Mr. Robert Day. The author's note declared him to be a professor of English at Washington College in Chestertown, Maryland. I was less interested in this author or his book than in the little college which I knew of for three reasons. First, this was the current home of the Associated Writing Programs, the nearest thing to a union for American writers. Second, the school offered an annual literary prize for the best undergraduate writing, a cash award that today would buy a well-equipped Mercedez-Benz. Third, the roughly 1000-members, faculty and students, of this lovely little college held an annual go-naked day. Maybe I thought that in picking up Day's novel the eccentric zeitgeist clearly in residence wherever Chestertown was might rub off on me. Nada, I am afraid.

Still, if you wait long enough good things do happen. Especially good when they are eccentric enough. More than two decades after my book purchase, Bob invited me to come to Washington College to read my poems. It was a pleasant enough experience, unremarkable except for meeting himself and his wife the painter Kathryn Jankus

Day, having a day of lively literary gossip, and feeling that extraordinary thing, the delight that comes with a sudden and solid friendship. Some of the best friendships are brief encounters, especially when they recur over time or distance or, in the poet's case, genre. The book you are reading, small and in its way unassertive, scores in all of those ways. It would be sufficient for me to say read this, an act of friendship.

Why, after all, do we read? I imagine hands going up to suggest the unimpeachable values of enlightenment, civilization, individual redemption, knowledge etc, and these enable, if they do not wholly exist as, pleasures at some level to all of us. Among those pleasures is gossip. These days gossip sounds like the dirt of which people are master-flingers and whackers. One definition of gossip is that it "empowers one person while disempowering another." But that seems an equal fit for the satiric delight in all jokes. Unless gossip is a malice-intended fabrication, which makes it a fiction, all gossip does is reveal. It exposes what we suspect but are not sure of, what we hope but deny we hoped, what we won't admit shocks us even as our mouths drop. Gossip is an intimate story. Flannery O'Connor's gossip, gathered in a production of books that is almost minimal, is like Kafka's gossip, always fresh and funny and hard-looking. Gossip can't be fooled. Writers love its heft and warp and sound because they delight in folly and are pledged to abhor sentimentality, that untruth. Unless you think of Dickens. Or Welty.

Well! as Jack Benny used to say. What he might have said is—what's the difference between gossip and memory?

Doesn't the latter turn into the former at some point in every life? Maybe the answer is fiction. Maybe it is what is now called life writing. Clearly, I don't know. But I have some ideas.

My idea today is that there is a form of literary writing which by any other name is gossip. It remembers, yokes up this and that, takes itself, well, not unseriously but rarely descends to somber pronouncement. It likes to sidle up with a joke, drop some names and places, insinuate softly. The best practioners really do know a few things it turns out we wanted to know, but it is their way of speaking to us, which separates the gold from the goldplate. Some writing has the delightful charm and hold of lunch with the kind of friend we can't imagine not having, once we have him or her. I go so far as to say there is a kind of gossip befriends us when we are the appointed recipient, which is different from being the impaled subject. The thing that makes this form of writing so attractive is the balance of light and heavy–or at least less light–wherein lies jarring contrast, contradiction, unequivocally and deftly revealed truth, whether apercu or long-winded epic anecdote. Here the truth, it turns out, is almost never what subject, person, or scene lies so revealed; it is the style, the character of the telling mouth, and we draw near because it is so, well, affably idiosyncratic. We like to say individual, but that isn't enough for Bob Day.

Bob grew up in Kansas with enviable sashays into much of exotic Europe. He knows horses, quail, flat-land farms, and distance. Contemporary European culture in all its ziggy cool is a patois to him. He has lived for years, part-and-full time in southern France, as well as eastern Maryland. His eye is as quick to seize on a remarkable detail as a swooning prairie hawk. He possesses an uncannily light touch in yoking together disparate places, people, and things. That is the form of gossip he practices in this tidy book. One sees it in his remark that from his Kansas he brought a knowledge of dry wells to lunch with his literary chum, redoubtable John Barth, who found Day's definition of a dry well and a continuously active one—a "gurgler" —apt descriptors for writers, some who don't do much and some who do a lot. Day has been, he admits, both but seems in recent days to be a steady and abundant producer, merely to judge from the short stories appearing in nice journals. The memoirs gathered here are not those splendid fictions. They are not precisely essays, nor are they the seedier, tackier forms of gossip that act as little mirrors for the self-attentive. They are, however, glimpses–sometimes more extended—sideways and fore and aft—which permit Bob to focus a brief, jaunty, knowing gaze on writers who have crossed his path. I happen to be one of those writers, so I have decided I have a special purchase in saying how sly and delightful this collection is.

Well.

Bob calls his pieces "Chance Encounters of a Literary Kind." Whimsy, I think. The poets and writers he attends to here seem not arrayed hierarchically nor, so far as I can tell, in any schematic pattern other than Bob's inscrutable interest. He treats Shakespeare, William Stafford, Mavis Gallant, John Barth, Ray Carver, Walter Bernstein, and Michael de Montaigne. His gathering of word folk has the sweet scent of memorial but there is also a brass-taste of reality and mortality stands always firmly in the room. It might be said Bob employs his scribes to offer, as he looks upon them, plain and good instruction in the art of writing. If so, it comes as more aside than soliloquy, is practical as an eraser and coffee and, anyway, what matters are the chronicles of surprises like unexpected dinner with Diane Keaton and Diane Carroll. Or finding Bob was the author of Willy Nelson's wonderful line about a woman who could suck the chrome off a trailer-hitch. The whole of the book takes about as long to consume as a double cheeseburger, fries, and two beers, a consumption less about the others in the picture than the Bob who brought us to his table. Bob's mind, and its book, is about pleasure, memory, gazing around, feeling how weird and yet how agreeable our time together is. Of course, that's what any memorable meal with a friend can be, and so often is not. Now I think about it, this is a portrait of friendship, among the toughest of subjects to get right. A tour de force, this patchwork of thought and feeling and grace, funny and spicy and sharp, makes me think again of Bob Day's friend, Jack Barth, who wrote "Self-knowledge is bad news." The icy truth. But, luckily it turns out, not always the truth. And not the only truth.

Maybe the bigger, stronger truth here is simply a plain record of friendship, which Bob treats with the respect a farm lad reserves for a steady horse or a yellow deux chevaux, if he happens to find himself living in Paris and happens to own one, as Day has done. One of his friends was the American poet William Stafford, also of Kansas. A man of firm posture, literally and metaphorically, Stafford famously said koan-like things a writer might take to the bank. So, says Bob, Mr. Stafford said: "Do it all and do it now." "The threshold is never so high as you imagine." "The beginning may not be the beginning. The end may not be the end." I knew Mr. Stafford a little, having gone up to DC to meet him when he was the standing US Poet Laureate at the Library of Congress. I was a would-be poet then serving in the US Air Force. He gave me lunch. I tape-recorded our conversation so I could re-listen and learn.

Mr. Stafford, I asked, do you have a line theory? Lines of poetry seemed to me both alive and mystically indefinable. He said, speaking slowly, "yes, I do." When no more came, my breath held until then, I said, "what is it?" He waited a bit. Then he said " I know I am going to come to the edge of the page and will have to turn, to start another line." I thought for years he was having me on, a subtle joke. But he was directing me as bluntly and efficiently as one could to the origin of poetic lines in the back-and-forth turn of a plow, to rhythmic inevitability and idiosyncratic innovation. An abidingly wise poet and a would-be at table, with iced tea glasses all sweating, a chance encounter with nothing at stake except maybe some long-range consequences nobody could predict or even manage to hope for. And here, forty-five years later, delight in that sweet moment of friend-making is all over me.

I don't say Bob's book will come to the same thing for those fortunate enough to come to it, but I wouldn't be surprised. I do say—for people who know what love and respect and imagination and honest candor are all in one place—this is gossip of the finest kind, and ready to hand as a Kansas wind or a Paris sidewalk with Mavis Gallant on Bob Day's arm. But the best piece is Day's memoir of his mother. I am writing this three days before Mother's Day of 2015, thinking of my late mother, longing some, cheered by the grit in that good woman, Mrs. Day.

Well, and that of her son Bob who brings us together.

Dave Smith
May 6, 2015

Authors' Notes

Robert Day's novel *The Last Cattle Drive* was a Book-of-the-Month Club selection. His short fiction has won a number of awards and citations, including two Seaton Prizes, a Pen Faulkner/NEA prize, and Best American Short Story and Pushcart citations. His fiction has been published by *Tri-Quarterly*, *Black Warrior Review*, *Kansas Quarterly*, *North Dakota Quarterly*, and *New Letters* among other belles-lettres magazines. He is the author of two novellas, *In My Stead* and *The Four Wheel Drive Quartet*, as well as three collections of short fiction: *Speaking French in Kansas*, *Where I Am Now, and The Billion Dollar Dream*.

His nonfiction has been published in the *Washington Post Magazine*, *Smithsonian Magazine*, *Forbes FYI*, *Modern Maturity*, *World Literature Today*, *American Scholar*, and *Numero Cinq*. As a member of the Prairie Writers Circle his essays have been reprinted in numerous newspapers and journals nationwide, and on such internet sites as *Counterpunch*. Recent book publications include *We Should Have Come By Water* (poems), *The Committee to Save the World* (literary non-fiction), and *Chance Encounters of a Literary Kind* (memoirs). Forthcoming publications include: *Let Us Imagine Lost Love* (a novel, Fall 1015), and *Robert Day for President: an Embellished Campaign Autobiography* (Spring, 2016).

Among his awards and fellowships are a National Endowment to the Arts Creative Writing Fellowship,

Yaddo and McDowell Fellowships, a Maryland Arts Council Award, and the Edgar Wolfe Award for distinguished fiction. His teaching positions include The Iowa Writers Workshop; The University of Kansas; and the Graduate Faculty at Montaigne College, The University of Bordeaux.

He is past Acting President of the Associated Writing Programs; the founder and former Director of the Rose O'Neill Literary House; and founder and Publisher of the Literary House Press at Washington College, Chestertown, Maryland.

Douglas Glover is the author of five story collections, four novels, two books of essays, *Notes Home from a Prodigal Son* and *Attack of the Copula Spiders*, and *The Enamoured Knight*, a book about *Don Quixote* and novel form. In 2007, he was given the Writers' Trust of Canada Timothy Findley Award for an author in mid-career. His novel *Elle* won the 2003 Governor-General's Award for Fiction, was a finalist for the IMPAC Dublin Literary Award, and was optioned by Isuma Igloolik Productions, makers of *Atanarjuat, The Fast Runner*. His story book *A Guide to Animal Behaviour* was a finalist for the 1991 Governor-General's Award. His stories have been frequently anthologized, notably in *The Best American Short Stories*, *Best Canadian Stories*, and *The New Oxford Book of Canadian Stories*. He was the subject of a TV documentary in a series called *The Writing Life* and a collection of critical essays, *The Art of Desire, The Fiction of Douglas Glover*, edited by Bruce Stone.

Dave Smith has published more than a dozen volumes of poetry, including *Little Boats, Unsalvaged: Poems 1992–2004* and *The Wick of Memory: New and Selected Poems, 1970–2000*, which was chosen as the *Dictionary of Literary Biography*'s Book of the Year in Poetry. Smith's prose includes the novel *Onliness* (1981), the story collection *Southern Delights* (1984), and the essay collection *Hunting Men: Reflections on a Life in American Poetry* (2006). He has received fellowships from the National Endowment for the Arts, the John Simon Guggenheim Foundation, the Bread Loaf Writers' Conference, the Lyndhurst Foundation, and the Rockefeller Foundation. He has twice been a finalist for the Pulitzer Prize.